Things She Wishes You Understood

Derrick Jaxn

Introduction

Communication is said to be a lost art. While I'd love to disagree, I personally know how it feels to have misplaced my brush in the pile of insecurities, brokenness, ego, pride, and self-centered way of thinking I once hoarded. Even till this day, I occasionally find my brush hiding somewhere under another box of unpacked internal baggage that has no place in a healthy relationship, nor a happy life in general.

Clearly, the turning point in my life wasn't in me becoming perfect, but rather having the wisdom to use my brush. To start having the difficult and sometimes painful conversations. To open up when my comfort zone was shutting down. To blame myself when I knew I was wrong instead of pointing fingers elsewhere when I knew I could get away with it. To speak up instead of letting passive-aggressive hints speak for me.

It wasn't rocket science. It was a choice life gave me, the same one it gives every man. Either wise up, grow up, and step up to the plate, or continue to avoid my demons, cling to my toxicity, and lose the woman who knew she deserved so much better.

Not only did I refuse to allow the latter, I bet my life against it, found my purpose in it, and now am writing this book with it. I've done the years of hard work so that some man who still has a chance to keep the love of his life can learn many of my lessons the easier and smarter way than I did. If not for him, then at least for the woman who's been trying to find the words to voice the intent of her intuition but couldn't, this is for you.

To my younger self, this is for you, too. You're not some ancient version of me I no longer must account for. You are every day that has something left to learn, to be mindful of, and to improve on in your ability to receive from your wife what she still needs you to understand to properly love the ever-evolving version of her.

The following passages are from conversations with my conscience over the last few years, derivative of uncomfortable relationship discussions I couldn't stop replaying after they were done. My conscience articulates many of the same things as other men, but for those who, like I once did, have difficulty hearing through the clutter left by mental adolescence, may these truths find you well and before it's too late.

She's not unforgiving,

but she might need some more

time and space to process your apology.

The damage doesn't become undone the

moment you realize you didn't mean to cause it.

-Derrick Jaxn

She's not looking for a savior.

She may not currently even be looking for

a solution. Eventually, yes, but right now

she needs your sympathy as evidence you're

more mindful about the way you make her

feel than you are about the way you'll "fix"

whatever consequences about how you made her
feel.

-Derrick Jaxn

She's not fishing for compliments;
she's reminding you to acknowledge how
attracted to her you are the same way you
remind her to ignore other men who show
they are attracted to her.

-Derrick Jaxn

You can't want her to be ambitious
without also wanting to be supportive
when she fails at the things, she's ambitious
about. Support is not just a "woman"
thing. It's a partner thing.

-Derrick Jaxn

She's not shallow for enjoying
gifts from you. They're representations
of the small sacrifices of time it took to
get them, and the hard work it took to
earn money to buy them that you were willing
to give in exchange for showing you were
thinking of her.

-Derrick Jaxn

Telling her you don't understand where
she's coming from, but asking for
her patience as you continue to try to
put yourself in her shoes is better than an
insincere apology just to shut her up.

-Derrick Jaxn

The time she needs for herself
is not a measurement of her
investment in you. Allow her the
space she needs for self-maintenance
without punishing her for the lack of
on-demand attention you want regardless of
her emotional needs.

-Derrick Jaxn

You can work on your dreams

without keeping her last

on your priority list. A better way

to integrate her into your life of

pursuing success is to set aside time

she needs from you to feel connected, and

commit to it with your undivided attention

when it comes.

-Derrick Jaxn

Yes, you told her you loved her.

You told her she was beautiful.

You told her how much she meant

to you, and how you see her in your future.

Now, you need to tell her, again.

Tomorrow, show her, and

the next day, repeat these steps.

Her memory shouldn't be the only evidence

of these things being true.

-Derrick Jaxn

She's not living in the past by bringing up
old events that brought her pain. The past
is living in her in the form of scars you caused
and receives new life with
every time you remind her of the person you
were when you caused them.

-Derrick Jaxn

She will support you in your hard times, when you're angry, depressed, or just frustrated. But to take these things out on her is to take away your own support while she emotionally protects herself. Don't blame her for the problems you added to.

-Derrick Jaxn

Yes, she can take a joke,

but once you're aware of certain

insecurities and you still choose to

poke fun at them, those jokes are more

inconsiderate than amusing.

-Derrick Jaxn

She wants you to put her on a pedestal,

but don't forget to put her flaws up there, too.

Don't be in awe of her only when she's at her best.

She needs a place to be less than perfect more than

she needs an admirer of only a small part of her.

-Derrick Jaxn

She doesn't mind making sure you're
taken care of,
but just because she's a nurturer
doesn't mean she doesn't deserve
nurturing as well.

-Derrick Jaxn

She doesn't mind the fact that
you're very sexual. You just also
need to be sensual,
respectful, and romantic. That
creates the intimacy that makes
the sex even better.

-Derrick Jaxn

No, she does not think she's
"all that." She thinks she has
a man who's secure enough in
himself and proud enough in
his woman to where her accomplishments
won't intimidate him.

-Derrick Jaxn

She's not looking for all your time,

and she knows that you work hard, so you

need to focus throughout the day.

But she also knows that if she really

crosses your mind like you cross hers,

a few seconds to text her,

despite not being able to chat for long,

isn't too much to ask for.

-Derrick Jaxn

The time she spends on herself

may not be solely for you, but

paying attention to detail will

make her feel a lot more loved

than criticizing her for it or accusing

her of doing it for superficial reasons.

-Derrick Jaxn

If you come home from having a bad day, no, you don't have to pretend. But that's not an excuse for shutting her out when she's only trying to see how she can help.

-Derrick Jaxn

Her career and educational
success is not indicative of a lesser
value on you. You've meant more to
her than your money from the beginning.
Don't let society's limitations on you as a
man convince you otherwise.

-Derrick Jaxn

Asking for more respect from you
is not a disrespect to you.
Having to ask for more respect
from you is going to eventually make
her create distance from you that you
will have to respect.

-Derrick Jaxn

Her having needs of undivided
attention from you doesn't make
her "needy." It makes her a woman
whose needs you had no problem fulfilling
when you still wanted her to be all yours.
If you cherish her, show her to let her know.
If not, stop wasting her time and let her go.

-Derrick Jaxn

The pride you show in her looks
is much appreciated, but the support
you say you have for her mindset
and character should be shown, too.

-Derrick Jaxn

Flirting with other women is
not a part of your personality.
It's a part of your disregard for your
woman's feelings about it.

-Derrick Jaxn

She doesn't want you to
agree with everything she says,
but she needs to know you respect
everything she says even if you don't
agree.

-Derrick Jaxn

She's not jealous or insecure about
you having female friends. But
your boundaries or lack thereof
don't warrant her comfort either.

-Derrick Jaxn

Her "nagging" you isn't
caused by her inconsideration,
but by your inconsistency.
Following through on your
promises is the way to solve that,
not playing the victim.

-Derrick Jaxn

Your good intentions are recognized,
but it's your actions she feels.

-Derrick Jaxn

She doesn't want to know your
every move. She wants to know
that with every move you make,
you're going to respect your
relationship and protect her heart.

-Derrick Jaxn

Whether she can or cannot
"handle" the truth doesn't
absolve you of your obligation
to be truthful.

-Derrick Jaxn

When you compare her to
other women, you're telling
her she's still competing with
other women. If she's still
competing, that means you're still
entertaining, and it won't be long
before she gladly forfeits and lets you
realize what you've lost.

-Derrick Jaxn

Sometimes, you don't understand her
and it may be because she's still trying to
understand herself. But it's not fair to make
her feel like she's wrong for being a work
in progress in that area when you claim to
be the same thing in several areas.

-Derrick Jaxn

She doesn't want your
free time. She wants time
reserved just for her, in advance,
uninterrupted, and without
having to ask.

-Derrick Jaxn

She doesn't want you to
"solve" her. Sometimes she
just needs you to listen and try
to feel where she's coming from.
You're her man, not her math teacher.

-Derrick Jaxn

She's not complaining.

She's not whining.

She's allowing you to be the
space where she can be vulnerable,
imperfect, and open about what's
going on with her internally. Making
her feel wrong for that is to shut
her out, and once she feels more warmth
outside than inside with you, there will be
no coming back.

-Derrick Jaxn

She doesn't need you to compete
with other men, but she loves when
you compete with your former self
to love her better than you did yesterday.

-Derrick Jaxn

She doesn't expect you to
be a mind reader; she expects
you to be a vibe reader. Her love
allows her to be that
for you when you don't have the
energy to both explain yourself
and maintain your sanity,
and it'd be nice if she got the same
love from you in return.

-Derrick Jaxn

She doesn't need you for
everything, but it'd be nice
to know she can call on
you for anything.

-Derrick Jaxn

She doesn't want you to
fix her life, but she would
like you to try and improve something.
Refusing to see her struggle
without doing something about
it is one of the most romantic things
in the world to her, no matter what
the outcome is.

-Derrick Jaxn

You're not wrong for
wanting to unwind after
being at work all day.
It just hurts her when you forget
she's been waiting to see you
get home from work all day and
you act like your video games or drinks
with your friends is more important
than her missing you.

-Derrick Jaxn

To cry in front of her
is not to appear to be
less than a man. It's to be
more of a man, a human, and
her partner, and she appreciates
it more than she can ever
put into words.

-Derrick Jaxn

She loves surprises,

but that doesn't justify a consistent

lack of planning. Before long,

your spontaneity

starts feeling more like you're

being inconsiderate, last

minute, and that to you,

she's just an afterthought.

-Derrick Jaxn

She doesn't expect you to get along

with every one of her friends and family,

but putting genuine effort into connecting with them

is going to help her build trust in your

long-term intentions.

-Derrick Jaxn

She doesn't love you for
the same reasons the
world does, so those
things that impress them
won't impress her. Yes,
she can appreciate all that
you've accomplished in
your career, but she cares
more about what you invest
into your home.

-Derrick Jaxn

A part of letting yourself be loved,
is letting the woman who loves you
in so she can do what she signed up
for. It shows her that she's earned
your trust that she won't hurt you,
and that you appreciate the fact
that she's one of the few who will
never betray that trust.

-Derrick Jaxn

Some offenses don't come
with a second chance to get it
right on the next try. It doesn't
matter how much you stress
her responsibility to forgive,
it will never give you the right
to risk hurting her again, so don't
blow it.

-Derrick Jaxn

She's not keeping score.
She's keeping in mind that
you've been taking more than
you've been giving, and if that
doesn't change, she won't be able
to give to you much longer.

-Derrick Jaxn

Giving her attention to your
children, first, is not putting
you on the back burner. It's
putting what should be a shared
priority in its proper place, and
should be met with a plan for
scheduling and cherishing
more time together, not guilt trips.

-Derrick Jaxn

She can handle constructive criticism.
But it's still your responsibility to say it
in a way that doesn't tear her down.

-Derrick Jaxn

Being the breadwinner
doesn't absolve you
of your responsibility to
respect her. Providing for her
doesn't justify trying to
control her.

-Derrick Jaxn

She doesn't mind being your biggest
supporter, but she will not be your
biggest enabler. Supporting you
also means stopping you from
doing things that aren't going to
support you reaching your full potential.

-Derrick Jaxn

As much as you may
want homemaking to be
her strength, make sure patience
is yours while she develops in
that area. Comparing her to other
women, including your mother, shows
that you don't realize her value outside
of home, thus evidencing that you take
those things for granted and don't
deserve them anymore.

-Derrick Jaxn

Her respect for you
is to be earned, not demanded.
If you don't feel you can get it by
simply being respectable, your job
is to leave, not intimidate her.

-Derrick Jaxn

Stereotyping her with "you women"
is the perfect way to be left without
one.

-Derrick Jaxn

She's going to speak her
mind, but when you ask her
how she's doing, it's her heart
that she needs you to listen to.
Those words will come from her
body language and her tone, not
her verbiage.

-Derrick Jaxn

It's understandable
that you want her to watch
her weight, but supporting her
in that is to be tactful, resourceful,
and positive. Not degrading, insulting,
and gawking at other women.

-Derrick Jaxn

She has no problem with

you enjoying your down time,

but when your only display of excitement,

passion, and commitment is for your

recreation and not your relationship,

it's a problem.

-Derrick Jaxn

She loves when you respect
her wishes, but it means twice
as much when you do things
without having to be asked.

-Derrick Jaxn

Your shortcomings aren't
what push her away. Your
lack of effort to improve
those shortcomings does.

-Derrick Jaxn

She can't appreciate your kind
heart for others if it equates to
disregard for the well-being of hers.
Being nice to the random girl who blatantly
disrespected your relationship is to be
cruel to your woman.

-Derrick Jaxn

Neither her body nor her love
are "escapes" from your
wounds. Heal them so
you can love her the way
you convinced her you would.

-Derrick Jaxn

Having her back doesn't
mean you're enabling her.
It just means you know how to disagree
without treating her like she's the enemy,
especially in front of others.

-Derrick Jaxn

She doesn't need everyone in your
life that was there before her
to like her. But on behalf of you, they
should respect her, and without her
having to speak up for herself to get it.

-Derrick Jaxn

When she stops 'fussing'.
When she stops 'whining'.
When she stops 'hounding' you
about the things you said you were
going to do but didn't is probably
when she also will stop caring about
whether you'll come around because
she's already walking away.

-Derrick Jaxn

Calling her crazy or
criticizing her inability to
handle stress isn't going to do
anything but push her away. If
you really want to show "tough love,"
take on some of her toughest tasks for
her, or take time out of your schedule
to break them down into smaller tasks
and organize them for her. That's love.

-Derrick Jaxn

She knows it's the truth
and that she needs to hear it
whether she likes it or not.
But you must consider the timing
in which you say it and around whom,
or else it sends a completely different message.

-Derrick Jaxn

She loves expensive gifts,

but working on yourself in

some areas you need to improve on

is the best extension of your love

you could ever gift her with.

-Derrick Jaxn

She values your perspective,

but she also values her intuition

and in learning to trust it, your perspective

won't always come first.

-Derrick Jaxn

She understands she has to be
smart with her money, but
pampering herself is a part of
what allows her to make the money
she's to be smart with. She deserves and
needs that to improve her finances.

-Derrick Jaxn

She knows you won't always

feel the same about things the way she does,

but sharing in her emotions from time to

time shows that you at least want to be closer

to her. Whether she's excited, intrigued, or even

concerned about something, your validation of those

feelings are reflection of your investment in what's going

on with her, and it can make or break the bond you have.

-Derrick Jaxn

She doesn't need you to
"put her in her place." She knows
where she belongs. She only needs you
to rise to her level, or work with her
so you two can rise together.

-Derrick Jaxn

She loves that you're willing to say
"thank you," but she needs that to come
in the form of action. She needs to see
that you've considered what it takes for her
to do for you and are willing to pitch in and help
her with things sometimes, or find ways to
keep her replenished.

-Derrick Jaxn

Yes, she knows she needs to speak
to the king in you, but she needs you
to speak to the queen in her, too.
Yes with your words, but also with your
actions. You can't call her a queen but
then act like she's your servant or ignore
her needs like she's your slave.

-Derrick Jaxn

It's not that she can't just
"let it go," it's that it has not
let her go, yet. Making demands that
she snaps her fingers and gets through
a process that's already painful enough
only hurts her and proves you really don't care.

-Derrick Jaxn

Being your "trophy wife" is cool,
but she doesn't just want to be
shown off because of her physical
appeal to others. She wants to be cherished
because of her sentimental value to you.
Above all, how you treat her behind
doors is what matters; the rest is just icing
on the cake.

-Derrick Jaxn

She's not bitter or resentful,
It's just the mistake she made
of being naïve, hurt, and she refuses
to make it again.

-Derrick Jaxn

It's not that she's fallen off

and no longer cares about how she looks,

she just needs you to care about how she feels,

first, before being critical about her appearance.

If you can help her solve that problem, it will

solve the rest.

-Derrick Jaxn

She doesn't mind you hanging
with your guys, but she doesn't
like how easily influenced you are by

them. If you can't even say no to them
wanting you to spend every minute with
you, who's to say you're going to say no
when they want you to act single like them?

-Derrick Jaxn

You shouldn't tell her she's
doing too much when the truth
is you still care too much about
what others think of what she's doing.

-Derrick Jaxn

Yes, she is willing to change in order
to love you better. Just make sure those
changes aren't selfish or demeaning, and the
effort to make them is reciprocated because
you aren't perfect either.

-Derrick Jaxn

She's not trying to "move too quickly."
She's just not seeing tangible progression
in the relationship from you and doesn't
have time to waste.

-Derrick Jaxn

Her desire isn't to intrude on
your privacy or be nosy.
Her desire is to know that
you will always keep it real
with her so she doesn't have to
seek out the truth on her own.

-Derrick Jaxn

She loves that you smell good,

are well-groomed, and dress well.

But there's nothing more attractive to her

than your effort to take care of yourself, mentally,

so you can be better for both of you, emotionally.

-Derrick Jaxn

She is appreciative of the little things,
but she shouldn't have to celebrate you for every
single one of them. If you're doing them for the
right reasons, you shouldn't require her too, either.

-Derrick Jaxn

If you see her limping,

offer to rub her feet.

If you see her hand on her lower back,

offer to massage it.

If you see her fold her arms because

she's cold, offer her your coat, or even

better, hold her.

A part of being her protector is

being her comforter, too.

-Derrick Jaxn

No, you didn't ask for her opinion.

But you do expect her to care for you,

and occasionally, that will come in the form

of an opinion she feels can help you, even

if you won't like it.

-Derrick Jaxn

A thoughtful text message is nice,
but a consistent phone conversation is
even better.

-Derrick Jaxn

She knows that she's enough for
one man. If you don't demonstrate
that she is enough for you, she will
find the one who will.

-Derrick Jaxn

She's not upset that women from your past
keep coming back.
She's upset that you keep opening the door
when they do.

-Derrick Jaxn

Your depression

Your anxiety

Your fears

Your worries

Your stresses, don't have to hide from her.

Let her listening ear and comforting shoulder

be the substitute for your vices. She may not

be able to heal you, but she can add to the environment

you heal in if you're courageous enough not to run.

-Derrick Jaxn

Don't avoid conflict for the sake
of avoiding discomfort. Sometimes
that's the price to pay to avoid heartbreak
and a relationship spent despising each other.

-Derrick Jaxn

She's not blowing things out
of proportion. You've just ignored
her the entire time she was trying to
let you know how she felt, and now
that she's not letting you ignore her any
longer, you can't handle it.

-Derrick Jaxn

Derrick Jaxn

She is not a buffet. You cannot pick from
her what you enjoy and then leave the rest.
Either you will be nourished by her in full,
or play over someone else's plate.

-Derrick Jaxn

Loving her is not a favor to her.

If it is what you asked for the opportunity to do,

it is what you should do and be grateful for.

-Derrick Jaxn

Yes, she plans to spend her life with you,
but she'd rather change plans than spend her
life waiting on you to want to spend your life with her.

-Derrick Jaxn

She likes your physical presence,
but it's your emotional presence
she fell in love with. If she can't have
that, then she doesn't want either one.

-Derrick Jaxn

Derrick Jaxn

Yes, she is committed to you,
but above all, she is committed to
inner peace, growth, and God.
Interfere with any of those,
and she will leave.

-Derrick Jaxn

She's not mad at you because you
need time to work on yourself,
she's hurt because you started her love
just to leave her alone with it.
She'd rather you leave her alone
from the beginning than make her hitchhike
in the cold because you need maintenance.

-Derrick Jaxn

No intimacy is better than
lazy, thoughtless, mundane
intimacy. Touch her skin like the
privilege it is to be able to. Your passion,
creativity, and effort to deliver more than
just the bare minimum is the body language of
a man who still knows her worth, and she needs
that from you.

-Derrick Jaxn

She's yours.

She's loyal.

Her love for you is real.

She has no plans on going anywhere,

but don't let that stop you from pursuing

her like she's still just one thoughtful love letter,

romantic date, or reminder that you adore her

away from being in your life.

-Derrick Jaxn

If you're fully capable of
loving her correctly,
waiting until she's done
begging you to will be too
late to prove it.

-Derrick Jaxn

Yes, she enjoys sex,

but it doesn't fix every

problem in the relationship

and it won't make the conversations

you two need to have go away.

-Derrick Jaxn

Preventative measures
earn her respect.
Reactionary excuses lose it.
You choose.

-Derrick Jaxn

When in doubt,

over-explain what's wrong.

Even if it doesn't effectively

get your point across, it'll show

that you're trying and usually,

that's half the issue to begin with.

-Derrick Jaxn

She'd rather you say what it
is you really want from the beginning
than try to just give her what you
think she wants and later back out
when it's time to deliver.

-Derrick Jaxn

Don't blame her for every little
thing just to prepare an excuse
to leave. When or if you're ready
to leave, it's best to just get it over
with instead of trying to paint her
as the bad guy, first, so you can look
like a victim.

-Derrick Jaxn

She knows two wrongs don't
make a right, but if she pulls
a you on you, don't act all sensitive
because you weren't sensitive when
you first did her wrong.

-Derrick Jaxn

Bad hygiene isn't "manly."
It's disgusting, repulsive, and
inconsiderate to her, especially
if you think she's going to come and
be physical with you.

-Derrick Jaxn

If you're the head of the household,
that doesn't make you more important
than her.

-Derrick Jaxn

She doesn't negate that your
upbringing wasn't the best;
she's just holding you accountable
for being an adult, knowing that your
actions were wrong, and taking full
responsibility to never do them again
or face the consequences.

-Derrick Jaxn

If your comfort zone doesn't
contain places she'd love to travel
with you, things she'd like to experience
with you, or feelings she needs expressed
from you, then taking a step outside of it
is only going to make her love and appreciate
you more. There's nothing to fear.

-Derrick Jaxn

The label you give her
will only mean as much
as you prove it does, every
day.

-Derrick Jaxn

Fronting on her when
people are around will
get you embarrassed. She
knows you better than your
own mother, and will keep your
secrets safe unless you try to make
a fool out of her when she's done nothing
but hold you down.

-Derrick Jaxn

That on-again, off-again being with
her because you need some time
to "think" will turn into
"Don't call my phone again"
quick.

-Derrick Jaxn

Asking you to be who
you presented yourself as
in the beginning is not asking
you to be perfect.
It's just asking you to be real.

-Derrick Jaxn

Yes, she likes dates.
No, she does not like
dates that are strung
to expectations of sex,
afterwards. Take her out
because you want to make
memories and get to know
her better, not because you're
horny.

-Derrick Jaxn

Being faithful isn't just about
the girls you don't fuck. It's also
about the girls you draw the line with,
girls you don't follow on social media,
the texts you do respond to and tell them not
to text you again, the calls you do answer and
tell them not to call again, and the friends you let
know that your girl is your priority, now. Not them.

-Derrick Jaxn

She doesn't require you to be rich

or to give her the world. She requires

you to be certain of your choice to be with

and grow with her. She requires you to have

discipline over your body. She requires you to

be honest, even when you're ashamed of your truth.

She requires you to be committed, even when it's difficult.

She requires you to be kind even when you're upset.

None of those things costs a dime.

-Derrick Jaxn

CPSIA information can be obtained
at www.ICGtesting.com
Printed in the USA
BVHW030336311221
625281BV00005B/186